RADIANCE OF
SAINTHOOD

The book was created in cooperation
with the Catholic Cultural Centre

Text

John Paul II

Photographs

Adam Bujak
Arturo Mari

RADIANCE OF
SAINTHOOD

RADIANCE OF SAINTHOOD

The Cracow Metropolitan, Cardinal
Karol Wojtyła with the Primate of
the Millennium, Cardinal Stefan
Wyszyński during the celebrations of
St Stanislaus on the Rock in Cracow
(1968). Behind them, Rev. Stanisław
Dziwisz, today's Cardinal, the
Metropolitan of Wawel City

Exhibition selection,
editing and concept
Leszek Sosnowski

Graphic design
Janusz Feliński

Cooperation in editing
Jolanta Lenard

Computer layout
of the album and the exhibition
Studio Białego Kruka
Patryk Lubas
Cooperation
Robert Wójcik

German translation
Adam Sosnowski

English translation
Eunika Bogucka
Aneta Ptak

In cooperation with
L'Osservatore Romano
Medienboerse

Distribution in cooperation with
the Catholic Cultural Centre

First edition
Cracow 2006

ISBN 83-60292-06-X

Meditations on the Need for Holiness

(...) 90. The call to mission derives, of its nature, from the call to holiness. A missionary is really such only if he commits himself to the way of holiness: "Holiness must be called a fundamental presupposition and an irreplaceable condition for everyone in fulfilling the mission of salvation in the Church."

The universal call to holiness is closely linked to the universal call to mission. Every member of the faithful is called to holiness and to mission. This was the earnest desire of the Council, which hoped to be able „to enlighten all people with the brightness of Christ, which gleams over the face of the Church, by preaching the Gospel to every creature." The Church's missionary spirituality is a journey toward holiness.

The renewed impulse to the mission ad gentes demands holy missionaries. It is not enough to update pastoral techniques, organize and co-ordinate ecclesial resources, or delve more deeply into the biblical and theological foundations of faith. What is needed is the encouragement of a new „ardor for holiness" among missionaries and throughout the Christian community, especially among those who work most closely with missionaries.

Dear brothers and sisters: let us remember the missionary enthusiasm of the first Christian communities. Despite the limited means of travel and communication in those times, the proclamation of the Gospel quickly reached the ends of the earth. And this was the religion of a man who had died on a cross, "a stumbling block to Jews and folly to Gentiles"! (1 Cor 1:23) Underlying this missionary dynamism was the holiness of the first Christians and the first communities.

91. I therefore address myself to the recently baptized members of the young communities and young churches. Today, you are the hope of this two-thousand-year-old Church of ours: being young in faith, you must be

Vatican, Encyclical "Redemptoris Missio", 7 December 1990

◄
The first beatification (1979)

like the first Christians and radiate enthusiasm and courage, in generous devotion to God and neighbor. In a word, you must set yourselves on the path of holiness. Only thus can you be a sign of God in the world and re-live in your own countries the missionary epic of the early Church. You will also be a leaven of missionary spirit for the older churches.

For their part, missionaries should reflect on the duty of holiness required of them by the gift of their vocation, renew themselves in spirit day by day, and strive to update their doctrinal and pastoral formation. The missionary must be a "contemplative in action." He finds answers to problems in the light of God's word and in personal and community prayer. My contact with representatives of the non-Christian spiritual traditions, particularly those of Asia, has confirmed me in the view that the future of mission depends to a great extent on contemplation. Unless the missionary is a contemplative he cannot proclaim Christ in a credible way. He is a witness to the experience of God, and must be able to say with the apostles: "that which we have looked upon...concerning the word of life,...we proclaim also to you" (1 Jn 1:1-3).

The missionary is a person of the Beatitudes. Before sending out the Twelve to evangelize, Jesus, in his "missionary discourse" (cf. Mt 10), teaches them the paths of mission: poverty, meekness, acceptance of suffering and persecution, the desire for justice and peace, charity – in other words, the Beatitudes, lived out in the apostolic life (cf. Mt 5:1-12). By living the Beatitudes, the missionary experiences and shows concretely that the kingdom of God has already come, and that he has accepted it. The characteristic of every authentic missionary life is the inner joy that comes from faith. In a world tormented and oppressed by so many problems, a world tempted to pessimism, the one who proclaims the „Good News" must be a person who has found true hope in Christ.

Vatican, Encyclical "Redemptoris Missio", 7 December 1990

▶
Assisi (1982)

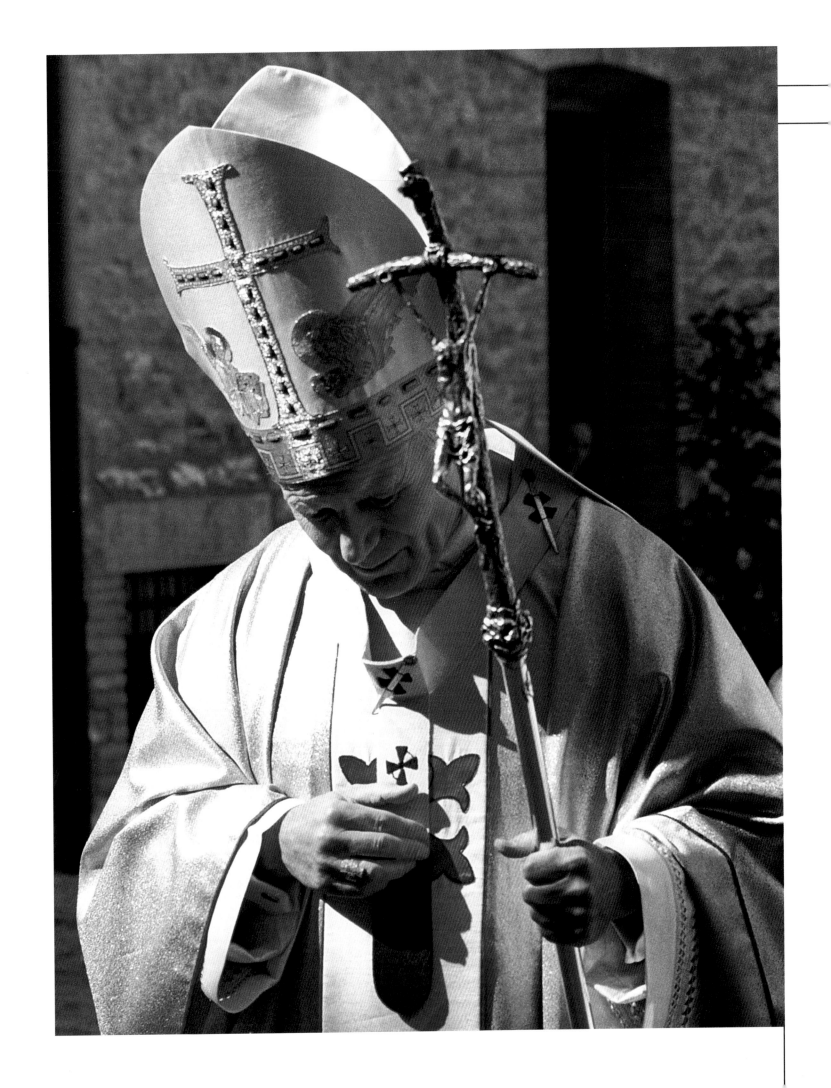

Christmas (1980)

With the Primate of Poland,
Cardinal Stefan Wyszyński
(1978)

Auschwitz,
the wall of death (1979)

Meeting with Polish people (1980)

Assisi – praying at the grave
with the reliquaries of St Clare (1982)

Midnight Mass (Christmas 1982)

Castel Gandolfo (1981)

Together with the Dalai Lama (1982)

Blessed be the Most Holy Sacrament ...
Vatican (1981)

Częstochowa, at the feet
of the Lady of Jasna Góra (1983)

Palace of the Metropolitan,
number 3, Franciszkańska Street
(1983)

Number 3,
Franciszkańska Street
(1983)

The Cracow Błonia – meeting
with former Auschwitz prisoners
(1979)

Poland, Katowice (1983)

Poland, farewell
at the Balice airport (1983)

A homily in the making (1984)

Sanctified Time of Illness

5. Address of pope John Paul II
to the pontifical council for health
pastoral care, 21 January 2005

(...)In her pastoral action, the Church is called to face the most delicate and unavoidable issues that well up in the human heart in the face of suffering, illness and death. It is from faith in Christ who died and rose that these issues can draw the comfort of the hope that does not disappoint. Today's world, which often does not possess the light of this hope, suggests solutions of death. Hence, there is the urgent need to promote a new evangelization and a strong witness of active faith in these vast secularized areas. 3. The Pontifical Council, therefore, does well to focus its reflections and programmes on the sanctification of illness and the special role of the sick in the Church and in the family, by virtue of the living presence of Christ in every suffering person. From this viewpoint, the year dedicated to the Eucharist is an appropriate opportunity for a more intense pastoral commitment in the administration of both Viaticum and the Anointing of the Sick. By fully configuring patients to Christ who died and rose, these sacraments enable sick persons themselves as well as the community of believers to experience the comfort that comes from supernatural hope.

Properly enlightened by the words of the priest and of those who assist him, the sick person can joyfully discover the particular mission entrusted to the sick in the Mystical Body of the Church: united with the suffering Christ, each one can cooperate in the salvation of humanity, making the most of his or her prayers with the offering up of one's suffering (cf. Col 1: 24).
 4. This must not, however, dispense Church leaders from paying stimulating and active attention to the structures where sick people sometimes suffer forms of marginalization and a lack of social support. Church leaders must also extend this attention to the areas of the world where the neediest of the sick, despite the progress of medicine, lack medical drugs and appropriate treatment.

▶

Archbishop Andrzej Maria Deskur
receiving his cardinal's hat (1985)

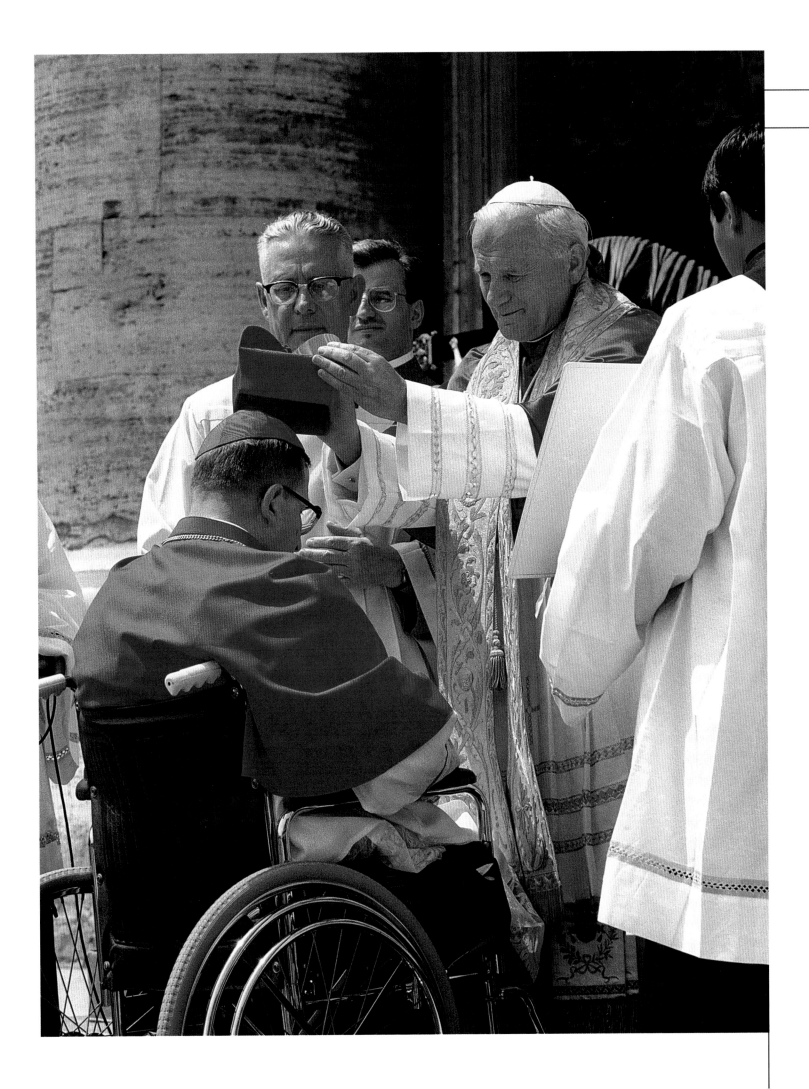

The Church must also devote special care to those areas of the world where those sick with AIDS receive no help. The Good Samaritan Foundation was created especially for them; its aim is to contribute to helping the peoples most exposed with the necessary therapeutic support.

The work of evangelization, the formation of consciences and the charitable witness that your Dicastery promotes in the world are a precious contribution, not only to comforting the suffering but also to guiding civil societies towards the demanding goals of the civilization of love.

5. I therefore thank you, dear brothers and sisters, for all the work done in these years, and I urge you to continue it with renewed enthusiasm. You know that I am constantly close to you and accompany you in your Dicastery's tasks with my prayers and my full confidence in the dedication you devote to your important activities. I encourage you in them, and to comfort you in your work I impart a special Apostolic Blessing to you, with which I also intend to embrace all those to whom you reach out through your work.

Address of pope John Paul II
to the pontifical council for health
pastoral care, 21 January 2005

◄
Palm Sunday (1985)

Castel Gandolfo (1981)

Christmas; Urbi et Orbi (1984)

Assisi, with the leaders
of world religions (1986)

Rome, vespers in the Saint Mary
Major Basilica with the Patriarch of
Constantinople (1987)

Cracow, the chapel in the
Archbishops' Palace (1987)

Poland, the Błonia Commons in Cracow (1987)

Poland, Jasna Góra (1987)

A Wonderful Holiday shall Shine

Homily at Mass and canonization of blessed Kinga
16 June 1999, Stary Sacz

1. "Saints do not fade away. Saints draw life from other Saints and thirst for holiness".

Dear Brothers and Sisters!

Almost thirty-three years ago I spoke these words at Stary Sacz, during the celebration of the Millennium. In doing so I made reference to a particular circumstance. Despite the inclement weather, the people of the territory of Sacz and the surrounding area had come to this city and that whole great assembly of the People of God, headed by the Cardinal Primate Stefan Wyszynski and the Bishop of Tarnów, Jerzy Ablewicz, prayed to God for the Canonization of Blessed Kinga. How then can I fail to repeat these words on the day when, by the decree of Divine Providence, it has been granted me to celebrate her Canonization, just as two years ago it was granted me to proclaim the sainthood of Queen Hedwig, the Lady of Wawel? Both came to us from Hungary, both entered into our history and have remained in the memory of the nation. Like Hedwig, Kinga has defied the inexorable law of time which erases everything. Centuries have passed, yet the splendour of her holiness has not only not faded, but it shines even more for successive generations. They have not forgotten this daughter of the King of Hungary, Princess of Malopolska (Little Poland), Foundress and Nun of the Convent of Sacz. And this day of her Canonization is a most magnificent proof of this. May God be praised in his Saints!

2. [...] May you be granted every grace by the One who is the the source and goal of all our holiness!

3. "Saints draw life from other Saints."

In the first reading we heard a prophetic proclamation: "You will shine with a glorious light to all parts of the earth; many nations shall come to you from afar, and the inhabitants of all the ends of the earth, drawn to you by the name of the Lord God" (Tob 13:13, Vulg.). These words of the Prophet

◀
Argentina, Buenos Aires (1987)

refer first of all to Jerusalem, the city marked by the special presence of God in his temple. Yet we know that, by his death and resurrection, "Christ has entered, not into a sanctuary made by hands, a copy of the true one, but into heaven itself, now to appear in the presence of God on our behalf" (Heb 9:24), and that this prophecy has been fulfilled in all those who follow him on the same path to the Father. Henceforth it is no longer the light of the temple of Jerusalem, but the splendour of Christ that enlightens the witnesses of his resurrection and draws to God's holy name the many nations and the inhabitants of all the ends of the earth.

Saint Kinga from birth had experienced in a remarkable way this saving radiance of holiness. For she came into the world in the royal Hungarian family of Bela IV, of the Arpad dynasty. This royal line was most fervent in the life of faith and gave rise to great saints. From it came Saint Stephen, the principal patron of Hungary and the son of Saint Emeric. A special place among the saints of the Arpad family belongs to women: Saint Ladislaa, Saint Elizabeth of Turin, Saint Hedwig of Silesia, Saint Agnes of Prague and finally the sisters of Kinga, Saint Margaret and Blessed Yolanda. Is it not obvious that the light of holiness in her family led Kinga to God's holy name? How could the example of her saintly parents, brothers and sisters and relatives, not leave a trace in her soul?

The seed of holiness sown in Kinga's heart in her family home found in Poland good soil for its growth. When she first arrived in Wojnicz in 1239, and then in Sandomierz, she established a warm relationship with the mother of her future husband, Grzymislawa, and with Grzymislawa's daughter Salomea. Both women were distinguished by deep piety, a life of asceticism and love of prayer, and the reading of Scripture and the lives of the saints. Their friendly company, especially in the first, difficult years of her stay in Poland, had a great influence on Kinga. The ideal of holiness increasingly

Homily at Mass and
canonization of blessed Kinga
16 June 1999, Stary Sacz

matured in her heart. Seeking models to imitate, corresponding to her rank, she chose as a special patroness her saintly relative Princess Hedwig of Silesia. She also wanted to hold up to Poland a saint who could become a teacher of love of country and Church to every state and region. Therefore, together with the Bishop of Kraków, Prandota of Bialaczew, she worked tirelessly for the canonization of the martyr of Kraków, Bishop Stanislaus of Szczepanów. A great influence on her spirituality was undoubtedly exercised by Saint Hyacinth, who lived during that time, Blessed Sadok, Blessed Bronislawa, Blessed Salomea, Blessed Yolanda, the sister of Kinga, and all those who created a particular faith-filled environment in the Kraków of those days.

4. In speaking today of sanctity, of the desire for and the pursuit of holiness, we need to ask ourselves how we can create environments which favour the aspiration to holiness. What can be done to make the family, the school, the workplace, the office, the villages and the cities, and finally the whole country a dwelling-place of saints, who can influence others by their goodness, their fidelity to Christ's teaching and the witness of their everyday lives, and thus foster the spiritual growth of all people? Saint Kinga and all the Saints and Blessed of the thirteenth century reply: it requires witness. It requires courage not to put your faith under a bushel-basket. And in the end it requires that in the hearts of believers there should abound that desire for holiness which not only shapes one's private life but also influences society as a whole.

In my Letter to Families I wrote that "the history of mankind, the history of salvation, passes by way of the family. The family is placed at the centre of the great struggle between good and evil, between life and death, between love and all that is opposed to love. To the family is entrusted the task of striving, first and foremost, to unleash the forces of good, the source of which is found in Christ the Redeemer of man. Every family unit needs to make these forces their own, so that, to use a phrase spoken on the occasion of the Millennium of Christianity in Poland, the family will be "strong with the strength of God" (No.23). Today, drawing upon the age-old experience of Saint Kinga, I repeat these words here among the inhabitants of the territory of Sacz, who for centuries, often at the cost of personal sacrifice, have given proof of their devotion to the family and of their great love for family life. Together with the Patroness of this land, I appeal to all my countrymen: May Polish families preserve their faith in Christ! Stand with firm perseverance at the side of Christ, so that he will remain in you! Do not allow the light of holiness to grow dim in your hearts, in the hearts of fathers and mothers, of sons and daughters! May the splendour of that light shape future generations of saints, for the glory of God's name! Tertio millennio adveniente!

Brothers and Sisters, do not be afraid to aspire to holiness! Do not be afraid to be saints! Make of this century now drawing to a close and of the new millennium an era of saintly men and women!

5. "Saints thirst for holiness". This thirst was alive in the heart of Kinga. With this desire she meditated on the words of Saint Paul which we have heard today: "Concerning the virgins, I have no command of the Lord, but I give my opinion as one who by the Lord's mercy is trustworthy. I think that in view of the present distress it is well for a person to remain as he is" (1 Cor 7:25-26). Inspired by this counsel, she sought to consecrate herself to God whole-heartedly by a vow of virginity. And so, when the circumstances of the time dictated that she was to marry Prince Boleslaus, she convinced him to live a life of virginity for the glory of God, and after a waiting-period of two years the spouses made a vow of perpetual chastity in the hands of Bishop Prandota.

Homily at Mass and
canonization of blessed Kinga
16 June 1999, Stary Sacz

Vatican, with Mother Theresa (1979)

This way of life, perhaps difficult to understand nowadays, yet deeply rooted in the tradition of the early Church, gave Saint Kinga that inner freedom which enabled her to be concerned first of all with the things of the Lord and to lead a profound religious life. Today let us reconsider this great testimony. Saint Kinga teaches us that both marriage and virginity lived in union with Christ can become a path to holiness. Today Saint Kinga rises to safeguard these values. She reminds us that the value of marriage, this indissoluble union of love between two persons, cannot be brought into question under any circumstances. Whatever difficulties may arise, one may not abandon the defence of this primordial love which has united two persons and which is constantly blessed by God. Marriage is the way of holiness, even when it becomes the way of the Cross.

The walls of the Convent of Stary Sacz, which Saint Kinga founded and where she came to the end of her life, seem today a testimony of how much she esteemed chastity and virginity, rightly seeing in this state an extraordinary gift whereby man experiences in a special way his own freedom. He can make of this inner freedom a place of encounter with Christ and with others on the path of holiness. Standing before this Convent, together with Saint Kinga, I speak in a special way to you young people: defend your inner freedom! Let no false shame keep you from cultivating chastity! And may the young men and women called by Christ to preserve life-long virginity know that this is a privileged state, which manifests most clearly the powerful work of the Holy Spirit.

There is yet another characteristic of the spirit of Saint Kinga, associated with her desire for holiness. As a princess she knew how to be about her Father's business even in this world. At her husband's side she shared in his rule, showing firmness and courage, generosity and concern for the good of the country and her subjects. During unrest within the state, during the

Homily at Mass and
canonization of blessed Kinga
16 June 1999, Stary Sacz

struggle for power in a kingdom divided into regions, during the devastating invasions of the Tartars, Saint Kinga was able to rise to the needs of the moment. She worked zealously for the unity of the Piast heritage, and in order to raise the country from ruin she did not hesitate to give away the entire dowry received from her father. Linked to her name are the rock salt mines of Wieliczka and Bochnia near Cracow. First and foremost, however, she was attentive to the needs of her subjects. The old biographies written on her confirm this, testifying that the people called her their "comforter", "physician", "nurse", "holy mother". Having renounced natural motherhood, she became a true mother to all.

She was also concerned for the cultural development of the nation. She herself and the local Convent are linked to the birth of true monuments of literature, such as the first book written in the Polish language: Zoltarz Dawidów, the Psalter of David.

All this is associated with her sanctity. And when we ask today how to go about becoming saints and living the life of holiness, Saint Kinga seems to reply: You need to be concerned with the things of the Lord in this world. She bears witness that carrying out this task consists in a constant effort to preserve harmony between the faith we profess and the life we lead. Today's world needs the holiness of Christians who in the ordinary conditions of family and professional life take on their proper daily duties, and who, in their desire to do the will of the Creator and to serve others each day, respond to his eternal love. This is true of the various areas of life such as political, economic, social and legislative activity (cf. Christifideles Laici, 42). These sectors must never lack the spirit of service, honesty, truth, and concern for the common good, even at the cost of an unselfish sacrifice of one's individual good, following the example of the holy Princess of these lands! In these areas too, may there be an abundant thirst for holiness, quenched by effective service in the spirit of love of God and neighbour!

6. "Saints do not fade away." As we look to the figure of Kinga, a fundamental question arises: What made her a figure which in a certain sense has not passed away? What enabled her to survive in the memory of the Polish people and, in particular, in the memory of the Church? What is the name of that power which defies the inexorable law that says, "everything fades away". The name of this power is love. Today's Gospel of the ten wise virgins speaks precisely of love. Kinga was certainly one of the wise virgins. Like them, she went out to meet the Divine Bridegroom. Like them, she kept watch with her lamp of love burning bright in order not to miss the moment of the Bridegroom's coming. Like them, she met him at his coming and she was invited to take part in the wedding banquet. The love of the Divine Spouse in the life of Princess Kinga found expression in countless acts of love of neighbour. It was truly because of that love that the "fading away" to which everyone on earth is subject has not erased her memory. Today, after so many centuries, the Church in Poland expresses that same love.

"Saints draw life from other Saints and thirst for holiness". Once more I repeat these words, here in the territory of Sacz. Kinga received this land as a gift in exchange for the dowry which she donated for the relief of the country, and this land has never ceased to be her special property. She always watches over the faithful people who live here. How can we fail to thank her for her care of families, especially the many local families with numerous children which we look upon with admiration and respect? How can we fail to thank her for imploring for this ecclesial community the grace of so many priestly and religious vocations? How can we fail to thank her for gathering us here today, uniting in common prayer brothers and sisters from Hungary, the Czech Republic, Slovakia and Ukraine, reviving the tradition of spiritual unity which she herself was so concerned to shape?

Filled with gratitude, let us praise God for the gift of the holiness of the Lady of this land, and let us pray that the splendour of this holiness will continue in all of us. In the new millennium, may this magnificent light shine to all the ends of the earth, so that peoples may come from afar to God's holy name (cf. Tob 13:13, Vulg.) and see his glory.

"Saints do not fade away".

Saints call upon holiness.

Saint Kinga, Lady of this land,

 Obtain for us the grace of holiness!

Homily at Mass and
canonization of blessed Kinga
16 June 1999, Stary Sacz

St Peter's Square,
Palm Sunday (1988)

The Dolomites, Lorenzago di Cadore (1988)

Santiago de Compostela (1989)

The gardens of Castel Gandolfo,
at the feet of Madonna (1989)

The Papal Gardens
of Castel Gandolfo (1989)

Wawel, in front of the Cross
of St Hedwig (1991)

Cracow, the chapel in the
Archbishops' Palace, in front of the
tomb of St Brother Albert (1991)

Wadowice, in the
parish church (1991)

Wadowice, the christening
bowl in the parish church (1991)

Vatican,
the private chapel (1993)

Vatican, Palm Sunday (2001)

With the Primate of Poland,
Cardinal Józef Glemp (1996)

Paris, with the young people
from all over the world (1997)

Valle d'Aosta,
vacation (1995)

Rome, the World Youth Day (1998)

The joy of meeting on Palm Sunday.
St Peter's Square (1984)

Poland, Wigry, with
the Milewski Family (1999)

St Peter's Square, the general
audience (1999)

On Mount Sinai (2000)

Bethlehem (2000)

Jerusalem – the Wailing Wall (2000)

The Coliseum – Stations of the Cross (2000)

Fatima – beatification of Jacinta
and Francisco Marto (2000)

St Peter's Square – closing of the
International Eucharistic Congress
(2000)

On holiday at Valle d'Aosta (2000)

Castel Gandolfo – Youth Jubilee (2000)

In the arms of the father,
the Holy Father. Tor Vergata (2000)

Echmiadzin, Armenia – at the memorial to the victims of the Armenian Genocide (2001)

Armenia, greetings
of Catholicos Karekin II (2001)

Echmiadzin, Armenia (2001)

Damascus, Syria – ecumenical
Holy Mass. (2001)

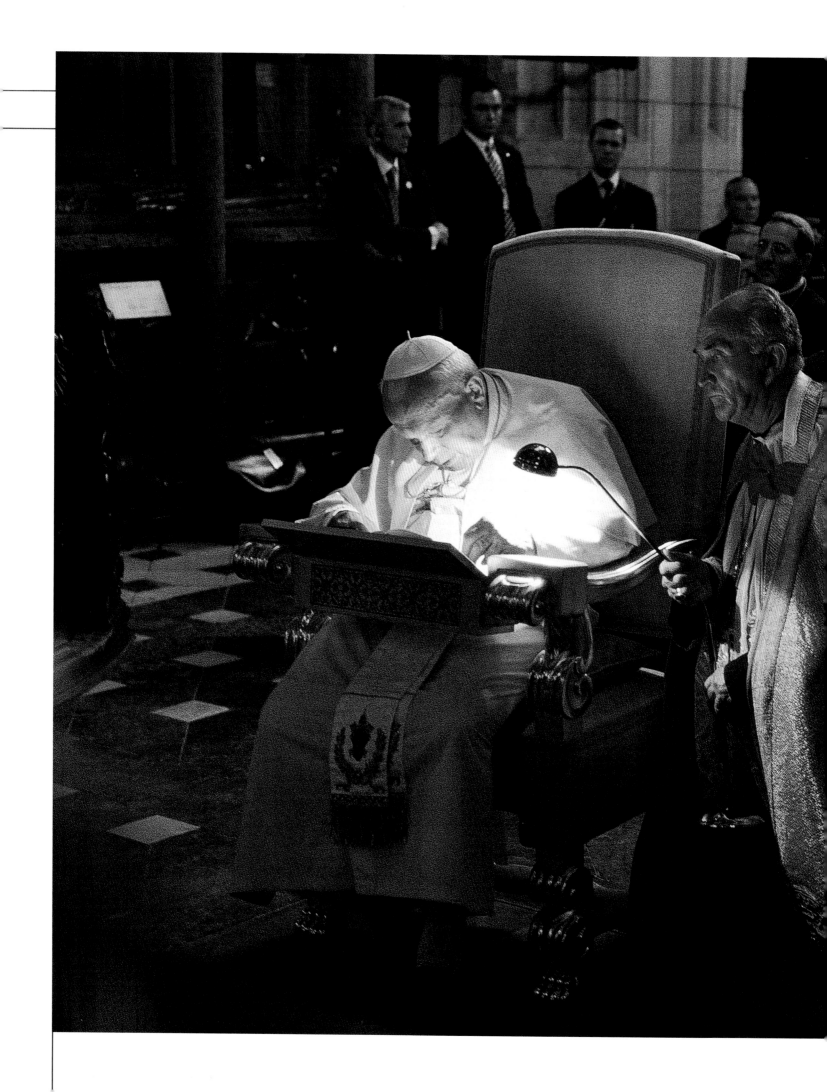

Cracow – praying
at the Wawel (2002)

Cracow, Łagiewniki
– the Divine Mercy Basilica (2002)

Cracow, Łagiewniki
– consecrating the Basilica (2002)

Kalwaria Zebrzydowska — in front of the
miraculous image of the Virgin (2002)

We Are Not the Sum Total of Our Weaknesses and Failures

Address of John Paul II to the bishops of California, Nevada and Hawaii on their „ad limina" visit, 14 May 2004

2. Every member of the Church is a pilgrim along the path of personal sanctification. Through baptism the believer enters into the holiness of God himself, being incorporated into Christ and made a dwelling place of his Spirit. But holiness is not only a gift. It is also a task, intrinsic and essential to discipleship, which shapes the whole of Christian life (cf. *Novo Millennio Ineunte*, 30). Impelled by the Lord's explicit teaching – „this is the will of God, your sanctification" (1 Th 4:3) – the community of believers rightly grows in the awareness that it is holiness which best expresses the mystery of the Church (cf. *Novo Millennio Ineunte*, 7) and which stirs the desire to give „striking witness" (*Lumen Gentium*, 39).

As Bishops you must be at the forefront of this spiritual journey of sanctification. Your episcopal ministry of ecclesial service, marked by your personal quest for holiness and your vocation to sanctify others, is a participation in Jesus' own ministry and directed towards the building up of his Church. It demands a pattern of life that unequivocally rejects any temptation to ostentation, careerism, or the recourse to secular models of leadership and instead requires you to bear witness to the kenosis of Christ, in pastoral charity, humility and simplicity of life (cf. The Code of Canon Law, c. 387; *Ecclesia in America*, 28). Walking in the presence of the Lord, you will grow in a holiness lived with and for your priests and people, inspiring in them the desire to embrace the high standards of Christian life and guiding them along the footsteps of Christ.

3. The credibility of the Church's proclamation of the Good News is intimately linked to the commitment of her members to personal sanctification. The Church is always in need of purification and so she must constantly follow the path of penance and renewal (cf. *Lumen Genti-*

um, 8). The Father's will that all believers be sanctified is amplified by the Son's fundamental exhortation: „Repent, and believe in the gospel" (Mk 1:15). Just as Peter boldly echoed this imperative at Pentecost (cf. Acts 2:38), you are charged with heralding a kerygmatic call to conversion and penance, proclaiming the boundless mercy of God, and inviting everyone to experience the call to reconciliation and hope at the heart of the Gospel (cf. *Pastores Gregis*, 39).

The courage to face the crisis of the loss of the sense of sin, to which I alerted the whole Church early in my Pontificate (cf. *Reconciliatio et Paenitentia*, 18), must be addressed today with particular urgency. While the effects of sin abound – greed, dishonesty and corruption, broken relationships and exploitation of persons, pornography and violence – the recognition of individual sinfulness has waned. In its place a disturbing culture of blame and litigiousness has arisen which speaks more of revenge than justice and fails to acknowledge that in every man and woman there is a wound which, in the light of faith, we call original sin (cf. ibid., 2).

Saint John tells us: „If we say we have no sin, we deceive ourselves" (1 Jn 1:8). Sin is an integral part of the truth about the human person. To recognize oneself as a sinner is the first and essential step in returning to the healing love of God. Given this reality, the Bishop's duty to indicate the sad and destructive presence of sin, both in individuals and in communities, is in fact a service of hope. Far from being something negative, it strengthens believers to abandon evil and embrace the perfection of love and the fullness of Christian life. Let us boldly announce that indeed we are not the sum total of our weaknesses and failures! We are the sum of the Father's love for us, and capable of becoming the image of his Son!

Address of John Paul II
to the bishops of California, Nevada
and Hawaii on their „ad limina" visit,
14 May 2004

4. The lasting peace and harmony so longed for by individuals, families and society can only be won through that conversion which is a fruit of mercy and constituent of genuine reconciliation. As Bishops you have the difficult yet satisfying duty of promoting the true Christian understanding of reconciliation. Perhaps no story better illustrates the profound drama of metanoia than the parable of the Prodigal Son, upon which I have elsewhere commented at length (cf. *Dives in Misericordia*, 5-6). The prodigal son is in a certain sense all men and women. We all can be lured by the temptation to separate ourselves from the Father and thus suffer loss of dignity, humiliation and shame, but equally so we all can have the courage to turn back to the Father who embraces us with a love which, transcending even justice, manifests itself as mercy.

Christ, who reveals the abounding mercy of God, demands the same of us, even when confronted with grievous sin. Indeed mercy „constitutes the fundamental content of the messianic message of Christ and the constitutive power of his mission" (ibid., 6) and thus can never be set aside in the name of pragmatism. It is precisely the father's fidelity to the merciful love proper to him as a father that sees him restore the filial relationship of his son who „was lost and is found" (Lk 15:32). As pastors of your flock it is with this merciful love – never a mere sense of favor – that you too must „reach down to every prodigal son, to every human misery, and above all to every form of moral misery, to sin" (*Dives in Misericordia*, 6). In this way you will draw good from evil, restore life from death, revealing anew the authentic face of the Father's mercy so necessary in our times.

5. Dear Brothers, I particularly wish to encourage you in your promotion of the Sacrament of Penance. As a divinely instituted means by

which the Church offers the pastoral activity of reconciliation, it is „the only ordinary way for the faithful to reconcile themselves with God and the Church" (Catechism of the Catholic Church, 1484). Though it cannot be denied that the profound power of this Sacrament is often considered today with indifference it is also the case that young people in particular readily give testimony to the graces and transforming benefits it bestows. Strengthened by this encouraging message I again appeal directly to you and to your priests: arm yourselves with more confidence, creativity and perseverance in presenting it and leading people to appreciate it (cf. *Novo Millennio Ineunte*, 37). Time spent in the confessional is time spent in service of the spiritual patrimony of the Church and the salvation of souls (cf. *Reconciliatio et Paenitentia*, 29).

As Bishops, it is of special importance for you to have frequent recourse to the Sacrament of Reconciliation in order to obtain the gift of that mercy of which you yourselves have been made ministers (cf. *Pastores Gregis*, 13). Since you are called to show forth the face of the Good Shepherd, and therefore to have the heart of Christ himself, you more than others must make your own the Psalmist's ardent cry: „A pure heart create for me, O God, put a steadfast spirit within me" (Ps 51:12). Sanctified by the graces received in your regular reception of the sacrament, I am confident that you will encourage your brother priests and indeed all the faithful to discover anew the full beauty of this sacrament.

6. With fraternal affection I share these reflections with you and assure you of my prayers as you seek to make the sanctifying and reconciling mission of the Church ever more appreciated and recognizable in your ecclesial and civic communities. The message of hope which

Address of John Paul II
to the bishops of California, Nevada
and Hawaii on their „ad limina" visit,
14 May 2004

you proclaim to a world often fraught with sinfulness and division will not fail to evoke fresh fervor and a renewed zeal for Christian life! With these sentiments I commend you to Mary, the Mother of Jesus, in whom is effected the reconciliation of God with humanity. I gladly impart to you and to the priests, deacons, Religious, and lay faithful of your Dioceses my Apostolic Blessing.

Kalwaria Zebrzydowska
– Holy Mass at the Basilica (2002)

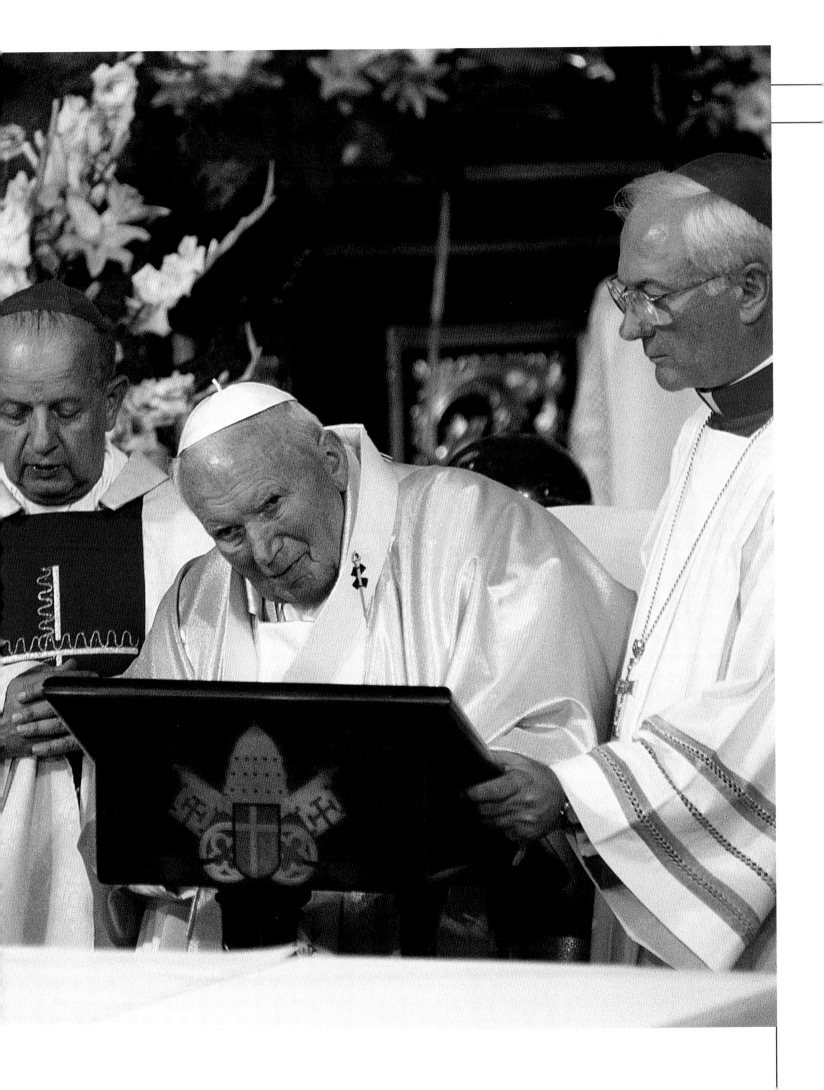

St Peter's Square – the beatification
of Urszula Ledóchowska (2003)

The beatification
of Mother Theresa (2003)

St Peter's Basilica celebrating
the feast of its patron (2003)

St Peter's Basilica — at the feet
of the crucified Christ (2004)

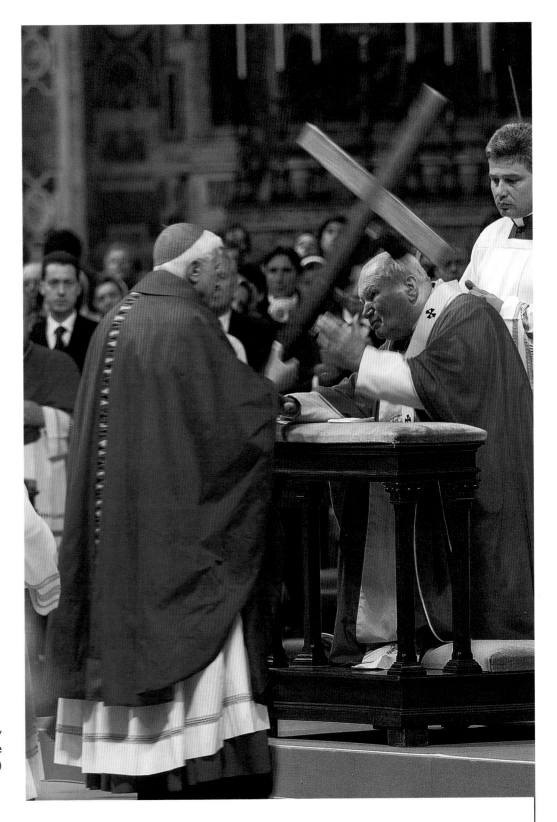

St Peter's Basilica, Good Friday
– cardinal J. Ratzinger holding the
cross for veneration (2004)

Testimony of the Holy Life

(...) 2. With his consecration, in fact, the Bishop fully becomes a teacher, priest and guide of the Christian community. Christ must therefore always be the heart of his ministry, the divine Teacher present both in the words of Scripture and in the sacrament of the Eucharist.

In the Apostolic Exhortation Pastores Gregis, I wanted to recall that the Eucharist is at the heart of the „munus sanctificandi" of the Bishop (cf. n. 37). I keenly hope that the Year of the Eucharist, which will begin on 17 October with the closing of the International Eucharistic Congress, will be a providential opportunity for examining more deeply the central importance of the Eucharistic Sacrament in the life and activity of every particular Church. It is round the altar that the bonds of fraternal love are strengthened and the awareness of all believers that they belong to the one People of God, whose Bishops are Pastors, is revived.

3. As Bishops it is your task to watch over the celebration of the sacraments and worship in general. Safeguard the expectations of the faithful to have a dignified celebration in which nothing is left to improvisation or chance. Indeed, the liturgy is the great school of Christian life where we worship, love and become acquainted with the Lord, where we are strengthened in our desire to follow the Teacher and in our determination to offer our own consistent witness.

You are, moreover, aware that the ministry of sanctification requires the witness of a holy life. The Spirit of God, who has made you holy through your episcopal consecration, expects of you a generous daily response. Your holiness is not merely personal, for its effects always prove beneficial to the faithful (cf. Apostolic Exhortation Pastores Gregis, n. 11), and imbues you with that moral authority you need to exercise your ministry effectively. The witness of our lives must confirm what we teach.

Address of John Paul II to the recently appointed latin and eastern rite bishops of territories under the jurisdiction of the congregation for bishops and the congregation for the oriental churches,
17 September 2004

◄
The Lourdes Grotto (2004)

4. Dear Brothers in the Episcopate, I exhort you to tend the flame of love for Christ at the altar each day, drawing from its heat the desire to give yourselves to God and to the Church.

May Mary, „Woman of the Eucharist", and the array of Apostles and holy Bishops sustain your steps and your ministry with their intercession.

With these sentiments, I impart my Blessing to you and gladly extend it to the communities entrusted to your pastoral care.

Address of John Paul II to the recently appointed latin and eastern rite bishops of territories under the jurisdiction of the congregation for bishops and the congregation for the oriental churches,
17 September 2004

▶
Good Friday at the Vatican
– private chapel (2005)

The Vatican – meeting the faithful
at the Angelus prayer (2005)

The Vatican window
– saying goodbye (2005)

The Vatican
– Clementine Hall (2005)

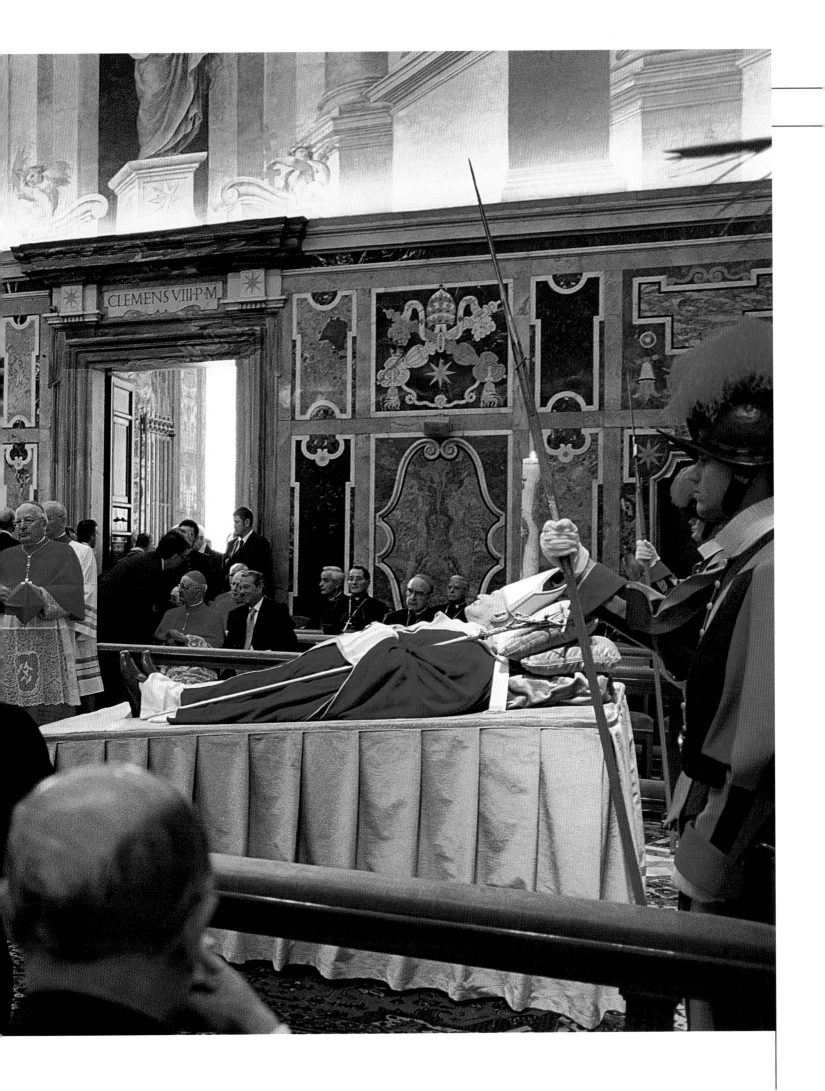

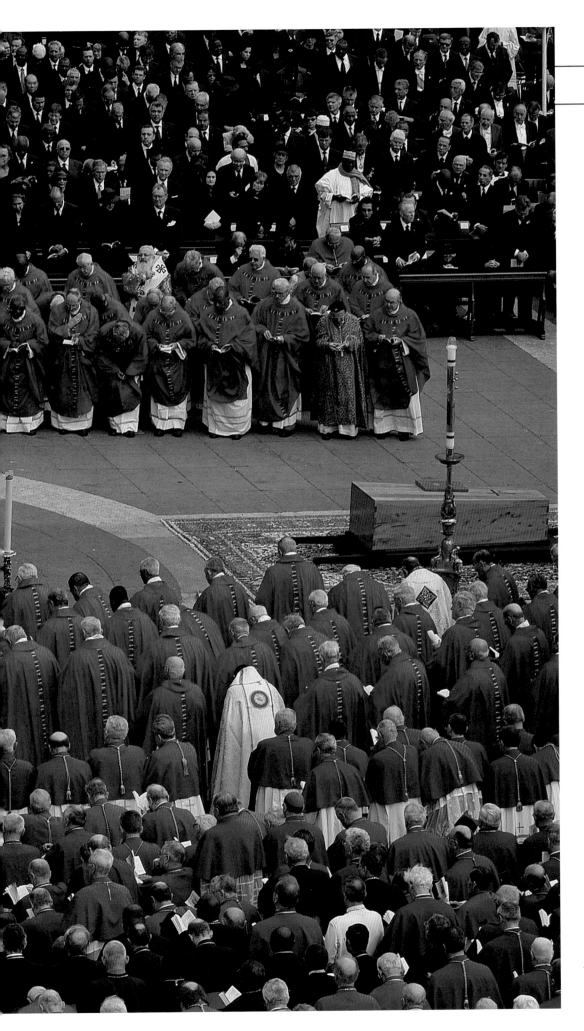

The funeral (2005)

Cracow – sorrow (2005)

Number 3, Franciszkańska
Street (2005)

Open-air exhibition „The Radiance of Sainthood" immediately
became an overwhelming experience for thousands of
Cracovians and Christians arriving from all over the world to
visit the beloved city of John Paul II (2006)

Under the displayed photographs
thousands of candles burn in
memory of and to honour the Holy
Father John Paul II
(2006)

St Peter's Square in a festive
anniversary mood (2000).

Biały Kruk Sp. z o.o.
ul. Szwedzka 38
PL 30-324 Kraków
tel./fax: (+48)
012 260 32 40
012 260 32 90
012 260 34 50
e-mail: biuro@bialykruk.pl
www.bialykruk.pl

First Edition
Kraków 2006

ISBN 83-60292-06-X